BOUND

A guide for the novel by Donna Jo Napoli
Great Works Author: Kristin Kemp, M.A.Ed.

Publishing Credits

Corinne Burton, M.A.Ed., *Publisher*; Emily R. Smith, M.A.Ed., *Content Director*; Lee Aucoin, *Senior Graphic Designer*; Stephanie Bernard, *Associate Editor*; Jess Johnson, *Graphic Designer*

Image Credits

p.22 Alatom/iStock; all other images from iStock and/or Shutterstock

Standards

© 2007 Teachers of English to Speakers of Other Languages, Inc. (TESOL)
© 2014 Board of Regents of the University of Wisconsin System, on behalf of WIDA—www.wida.us
© Copyright 2010. National Governors Association Center for Best Practices and Council of Chief State School Officers. All rights reserved.
ISTE Standards for Students, ©2016, ISTE® (International Society for Technology in Education), iste.org. All rights reserved.
© Copyright 2007–2018 Texas Education Association (TEA). All rights reserved.

Shell Education
A division of Teacher Created Materials
5301 Oceanus Drive
Huntington Beach, CA 92649-1030
www.tcmpub.com/shell-education
ISBN: 978-1-4258-1769-5
© 2018 Shell Educational Publishing, Inc.

The classroom teacher may reproduce copies of materials in this book for classroom use only. The reproduction of any part for an entire school or school system is strictly prohibited. No part of this publication may be transmitted, stored, or recorded in any form without written permission from the publisher.

Website addresses included in this book are public domain and may be subject to changes or alterations of content after publication of this product. Shell Educational Publishing does not take responsibility for the future accuracy or relevance and appropriateness of website addresses included in this book. Please contact the company if you come across any inappropriate or inaccurate website addresses, and they will be corrected in product reprints.

Table of Contents

How to Use This Literature Guide 4
    Theme Thoughts 4
    Vocabulary 5
    Analyzing the Literature 6
    Reader Response 6
    Close Reading the Literature 6
    Making Connections 7
    Creating with Story Elements 7
    Culminating Activity 8
    Comprehension Assessment 8
    Response to Literature 8

Correlation to the Standards 8
    Purpose and Intent of Standards 8
    How to Find Standards Correlations 8
    Standards Correlation Chart 9
    TESOL and WIDA Standards 10

About the Author—Donna Jo Napoli 11
    Possible Texts for Text Comparisons 11

Book Summary of *Bound* 12
    Cross-Curricular Connection 12
    Possible Texts for Text Sets 12

Teacher Plans and Student Pages 13
    Pre-Reading Theme Thoughts 13
    Section 1: Chapters 1–7 14
    Section 2: Chapters 8–13 24
    Section 3: Chapters 14–17 34
    Section 4: Chapters 18–23 44
    Section 5: Chapters 24–29 54

Post-Reading Activities 64
    Post-Reading Theme Thoughts 64
    Culminating Activity: One Story, Many Cinderellas 65
    Comprehension Assessment 67
    Response to Literature: Still Bound 69

Answer Key 71

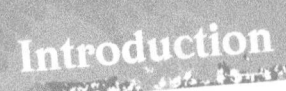

How to Use This Literature Guide

Today's standards demand rigor and relevance in the reading of complex texts. The units in this series guide teachers in a rich and deep exploration of worthwhile works of literature for classroom study. The most rigorous instruction can also be interesting and engaging!

Many current strategies for effective literacy instruction have been incorporated into these instructional guides for literature. Throughout the units, text-dependent questions are used to determine comprehension of the book as well as student interpretation of the vocabulary words. The books chosen for the series are complex exemplars of carefully crafted works of literature. Close reading is used throughout the units to guide students toward revisiting the text and using textual evidence to respond to prompts orally and in writing. Students must analyze the story elements in multiple assignments for each section of the book. All of these strategies work together to rigorously guide students through their study of literature.

The next few pages will make clear how to use this guide for a purposeful and meaningful literature study. Each section of this guide is set up in the same way to make it easier for you to implement the instruction in your classroom.

Theme Thoughts

The great works of literature used throughout this series have important themes that have been relevant to people for many years. Many of the themes will be discussed during the various sections of this instructional guide. However, it would also benefit students to have independent time to think about the key themes of the novel.

Before students begin reading, have them complete *Pre-Reading Theme Thoughts* (page 13). This graphic organizer will allow students to think about the themes outside the context of the story. They'll have the opportunity to evaluate statements based on important themes and defend their opinions. Be sure to have students keep their papers for comparison to the *Post-Reading Theme Thoughts* (page 64). This graphic organizer is similar to the pre-reading activity. However, this time, students will be answering the questions from the point of view of one of the characters in the novel. They have to think about how the character would feel about each statement and defend their thoughts. To conclude the activity, have students compare what they thought about the themes before they read the novel to what the characters discovered during the story.

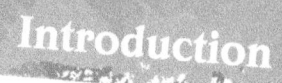

How to Use This Literature Guide (cont.)

Vocabulary

Each teacher overview page has definitions and sentences about how key vocabulary words are used in the section. These words should be introduced and discussed with students. There are two student vocabulary activity pages in each section. On the first page, students are asked to define the ten words chosen by the author of this unit. On the second page in most sections, each student will select at least eight words that he or she finds interesting or difficult. For each section, choose one of these pages for your students to complete. With either assignment, you may want to have students get into pairs to discuss the meanings of the words. Allow students to use reference guides to define the words. Monitor students to make sure the definitions they have found are accurate and relate to how the words are used in the text.

On some of the vocabulary student pages, students are asked to answer text-related questions about the vocabulary words. The following question stems will help you create your own vocabulary questions if you'd like to extend the discussion.

- How does this word describe _____'s character?
- In what ways does this word relate to the problem in this story?
- How does this word help you understand the setting?
- In what ways is this word related to the story's solution?
- Describe how this word supports the novel's theme of . . . .
- What visual images does this word bring to your mind?
- For what reasons might the author have chosen to use this particular word?

At times, more work with the words will help students understand their meanings. The following quick vocabulary activities are a good way to further study the words.

- Have students practice their vocabulary and writing skills by creating sentences and/or paragraphs in which multiple vocabulary words are used correctly and with evidence of understanding.
- Students can play vocabulary concentration. Students make a set of cards with the words and a separate set of cards with the definitions. Then, students lay the cards out on the table and play concentration. The goal of the game is to match vocabulary words with their definitions.
- Students can create word journal entries about the words. Students choose words they think are important and then describe why they think each word is important within the novel.

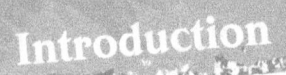

How to Use This Literature Guide (cont.)

Analyzing the Literature

After students have read each section, hold small-group or whole-class discussions. Questions are written at two levels of complexity to allow you to decide which questions best meet the needs of your students. The Level 1 questions are typically less abstract than the Level 2 questions. Level 1 is indicated by a square, while Level 2 is indicated by a triangle. These questions focus on the various story elements, such as character, setting, and plot. Student pages are provided if you want to assign these questions for individual student work before your group discussion. Be sure to add further questions as your students discuss what they've read. For each question, a few key points are provided for your reference as you discuss the novel with students.

Reader Response

In today's classrooms, there are often great readers who are below-average writers. So much time and energy is spent in classrooms getting students to read on grade level that little time is left to focus on writing skills. To help teachers include more writing in their daily literacy instruction, each section of this guide has a literature-based reader response prompt. Each of the three genres of writing is used in the reader responses within this guide: narrative, informative/explanatory, and opinion/argument. Students have a choice between two prompts for each reader response. One response requires students to make connections between the reading and their own lives. The other prompt requires students to determine text-to-text connections or connections within the text.

Close Reading the Literature

Within each section, students are asked to closely reread a short section of text. Since some versions of the novels have different page numbers, the selections are described by chapter and location, along with quotations to guide the readers. After each close reading, there are text-dependent questions to be answered by students.

Encourage students to read each question one at a time and then go back to the text and discover the answer. Work with students to ensure that they use the text to determine their answers rather than making unsupported inferences. Once students have answered the questions, discuss what they discovered. Suggested answers are provided in the answer key.

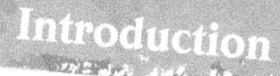

How to Use This Literature Guide (cont.)

Close Reading the Literature (cont.)

The generic, open-ended stems below can be used to write your own text-dependent questions if you would like to give students more practice.

- Give evidence from the text to support . . . .
- Justify your thinking using textual evidence about . . . .
- Find evidence to support your conclusions about . . . .
- What textual evidence helps the reader understand . . . ?
- Use the book to tell why _____ happens.
- Based on events in the story, ...
- Use text evidence to describe why . . . .

Making Connections

The activities in this section help students make cross-curricular connections to writing, mathematics, science, social studies, or the fine arts. Each of these types of activities requires higher-order thinking skills from students.

Creating with the Story Elements

It is important to spend time discussing the common story elements in literature. Understanding the characters, setting, and plot can increase students' comprehension and appreciation of the story. If teachers discuss these elements daily, students will more likely internalize the concepts and look for the elements in their independent reading. Another important reason for focusing on the story elements is that students will be better writers if they think about how the stories they read are constructed.

Students are given three options for working with the story elements. They are asked to create something related to the characters, setting, or plot of the novel. Students are given a choice in this activity so that they can decide to complete the activity that most appeals to them. Different multiple intelligences are used so that the activities are diverse and interesting to all students.

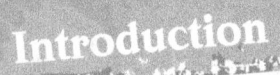

How to Use This Literature Guide (cont.)

Culminating Activity

This open-ended, cross-curricular activity requires higher-order thinking and allows for a creative product. Students will enjoy getting the chance to share what they have discovered through reading the novel. Be sure to allow them enough time to complete the activity at school or home.

Comprehension Assessment

The questions in this section are modeled after current standardized tests to help students analyze what they've read and prepare for tests they may see in their classrooms. The questions are dependent on the text and require critical-thinking skills to answer.

Response to Literature

The final post-reading activity is an essay based on the text that also requires further research by students. This is a great way to extend this book into other curricular areas. A suggested rubric is provided for teacher reference.

Correlation to the Standards

Shell Education is committed to producing educational materials that are research and standards based. As part of this effort, we have correlated all of our products to the academic standards of all 50 states, the District of Columbia, the Department of Defense Dependents Schools, and all Canadian provinces.

Purpose and Intent of Standards

The Every Student Succeeds Act (ESSA) mandates that all states adopt challenging academic standards that help students meet the goal of college and career readiness. While many states already adopted academic standards prior to ESSA, the act continues to hold states accountable for detailed and comprehensive standards. Standards are statements that describe the criteria necessary for students to meet specific academic goals. They define the knowledge, skills, and content students should acquire at each level. State standards are used in the development of our products, so educators can be assured they meet state academic requirements.

How to Find Standards Correlations

To print a customized correlation report of this product for your state, visit our website at www.teachercreatedmaterials.com/administrators/correlations/ and follow the online directions. If you require assistance in printing correlation reports, please contact our Customer Service Department at 1-877-777-3450.

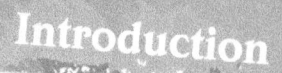

Correlation to the Standards

Standards Correlation Chart

College and Career Readiness Anchor Standard	Section
Read closely to determine what the text says explicitly and to make logical inferences from it; cite specific textual evidence when writing or speaking to support conclusions drawn from the text.	Analyzing the Literature Sections 1–5; Close Reading the Literature Sections 1–5; Making Connections Section 1; Response to Literature
Determine central ideas or themes of a text and analyze their development; summarize the key supporting details and ideas.	Analyzing the Literature Sections 1–5; Reader Response Sections 1–5; Making Connections Section 1; Creating with the Story Elements Section 3; Response to Literature
Analyze how and why individuals, events, or ideas develop and interact over the course of a text.	Analyzing the Literature Sections 1–5
Interpret words and phrases as they are used in a text, including determining technical, connotative, and figurative meanings, and analyze how specific word choices shape meaning or tone.	Vocabulary Sections 1–5; Making Connections Section 2
Analyze how two or more texts address similar themes or topics in order to build knowledge or to compare the approaches the authors take.	Culminating Activity
Read and comprehend complex literary and informational texts independently and proficiently.	Analyzing the Literature Sections 1–5; Reader Response Sections 1–5; Close Reading the Literature Sections 1–5; Response to Literature
Write arguments to support claims in an analysis of substantive topics or texts using valid reasoning and relevant and sufficient evidence.	Reader Response Sections 1, 3–4; Response to Literature
Write informative/explanatory texts to examine and convey complex ideas and information clearly and accurately through the effective selection, organization, and analysis of content.	Reader Response Sections 2, 4–5; Response to Literature
Write narratives to develop real or imagined experiences or events using effective technique, well-chosen details and well-structured event sequences.	Reader Response Sections 1–3, 5; Making Connections Section 4; Creating with the Story Elements Sections 4–5; Culminating Activity
Produce clear and coherent writing in which the development, organization, and style are appropriate to task, purpose, and audience.	Reader Response Sections 1–5; Culminating Activity; Response to Literature
Develop and strengthen writing as needed by planning, revising, editing, rewriting, or trying a new approach.	Culminating Activity; Response to Literature
Conduct short as well as more sustained research projects based on focused questions, demonstrating understanding of the subject under investigation.	Making Connections Section 3; Culminating Activity; Response to Literature
Draw evidence from literary or informational texts to support analysis, reflection, and research.	Culminating Activity

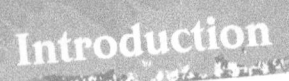

Correlation to the Standards (cont.)

Standards Correlation Chart (cont.)

College and Career Readiness Anchor Standard	Section
Demonstrate command of the conventions of standard English grammar and usage when writing or speaking.	Reader Response Sections 1–5; Close Reading the Literature Sections 1–5; Culminating Activity; Response to Literature
Demonstrate command of the conventions of standard English capitalization, punctuation, and spelling when writing.	Reader Response Sections 1–5; Close Reading the Literature Sections 1–5; Culminating Activity; Response to Literature
Apply knowledge of language to understand how language functions in different contexts, to make effective choices for meaning or style, and to comprehend more fully when reading or listening.	Reader Response Sections 1–5; Making Connections Section 2; Response to Literature
Determine or clarify the meaning of unknown and multiple-meaning words and phrases by using context clues, analyzing meaningful word parts, and consulting general and specialized reference materials, as appropriate.	Vocabulary Sections 1–5
Demonstrate understanding of figurative language, word relationships, and nuances in word meanings.	Making Connections Section 2
Acquire and use accurately a range of general academic and domain-specific words and phrases sufficient for reading, writing, speaking, and listening at the college and career readiness level; demonstrate independence in gathering vocabulary knowledge when encountering an unknown term important to comprehension or expression.	Vocabulary Sections 1–5
Acquire and use accurately a range of general academic and domain-specific words and phrases sufficient for reading, writing, speaking, and listening at the college and career readiness level; demonstrate independence in gathering vocabulary knowledge when encountering an unknown term important to comprehension or expression.	Vocabulary Sections 1–5

TESOL and WIDA Standards

The lessons in this book promote English language development for English language learners. The following TESOL and WIDA English Language Development Standards are addressed through the activities in this book:

- Standard 1: English language learners communicate for social and instructional purposes within the school setting.
- Standard 2: English language learners communicate information, ideas and concepts necessary for academic success in the content area of language arts.

About the Author—Donna Jo Napoli

As a child, Donna Jo Napoli never dreamed she would become an author. She grew up in an Italian-American family in Miami, Florida. Her father often gambled away their money, and the family had nowhere to live. Though she loved books and enjoyed escaping into the worlds they created, she wanted a career with financial security.

Napoli was an amazing student and went to Harvard University, earning a degree in mathematics in 1970. Three years later, she earned her Ph.D. in Romance languages from Harvard as well. Then, she did one year of post-doctoral studies in linguistics at Massachusetts Institute of Technology (MIT). After she finished her education, she settled into a career as a professor of linguistics at several universities in both the United States and abroad. She wrote five books on the subject and became a tenured professor at the University of Michigan.

Secure in her career, she began writing stories. After many rejections, Napoli published her first children's book called *The Hero of Barletta* in 1998. Her first book for young adults was *The Magic Circle* in 1993. Her books are varied in topics, ranging from realistic fiction to fantasy. She has also written several books with cultural or alternate versions of fairy tales. Her books have received many awards.

Napoli lives with her husband outside Pittsburgh, Pennsylvania. They have five children and a growing number of grandchildren. She is a naturalist at heart and loves to bake bread and garden.

Possible Texts for Text Comparisons

Other books authored by Donna Jo Napoli could be used as enriching text comparisons. Titles include *The Magic Circle*, *Breath*, and *Zel*. These books reimagine the fairy tales of Hansel and Gretel, the Pied Piper, and Rapunzel. *Ella Enchanted* by Gail Carson Levine could also be used as an alternative version of the Cinderella story.

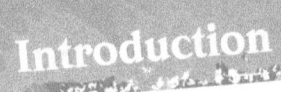

Book Summary of *Bound*

In this Cinderella tale set during the Chinese Ming Dynasty (1368–1644), the main character and her sister are both bound. Xing Xing (pronounced "Shing Shing") lives with her half-sister, Wei Ping, and her stepmother. Without a mother or father to help find her a husband, Xing Xing is bound to Stepmother for shelter and security, even though it means being emotionally abused and doing all the chores. Wei Ping's feet are bound, a painful process meant to shrink a woman's feet to the desirable size of a lotus blossom.

Xing Xing's life is very bleak, but a few things do bring her joy. She loves to do calligraphy, an unusual talent for a woman. Her neighbors, Master Tang and his wife, are kind to her and support her talent for composing poetry. When Stepmother sends Xing Xing to find medicine for Wei Ping's feet, she learns to open up and share her story with Yao Wang, a traveling doctor. She also forms a special relationship with a beautiful fish, who she believes is the reincarnation of her mother.

After a terrible loss and unexpected gifts, Xing Xing takes control of her own life and attends the cave festival in disguise. There, she is exposed to the possibilities of the world outside her own little village and longs to travel and explore. She is almost discovered by Stepmother and Wei Ping, so she makes a hasty retreat and leaves behind one golden shoe. It is sold to a prince who comes looking for its owner to become his wife. After a playful and honest conversation, the prince offers Xing Xing his hand. She happily accepts, feeling they will grow to cherish each other.

Cross-Curricular Connection

This book could be used in social studies units about Chinese culture/stories or women's rights, or a language arts unit about different versions of fairy tales.

Possible Texts for Text Sets

- Brown, Dinah. 2015. *Who is Malala Yousafzai?* New York: Penguin Workshop.
- Colson, Mary. 2012. *Chinese Culture*. Portsmouth: Heinemann.
- Louie, Ai-Ling. 1996. *Yeh-Shen: A Cinderella Story from China*. New York: Puffin Books.
- McCann, Michelle Roehm and Amelie Welden. 2012. *Girls Who Rocked the World: Heroines from Joan of Arc to Mother Teresa*. New York: Aladdin/Beyond Words.

Name _____

Date _____

Introduction

Pre-Reading Theme Thoughts

Directions: Read each of the statements in the first column. Decide if you agree or disagree with the statements. Record your opinion by marking an *X* in Agree or Disagree for each statement. Explain your choices in the fourth column. There are no right or wrong answers.

Statement	Agree	Disagree	Explain Your Answer
You should be kind to people even if they are not kind to you.			
It is okay for beauty to be painful.			
The most important thing is to take care of your family.			
Family members who have died can still be with you.			

© Shell Education   51769—Instructional Guide: Bound   13

Section 1
Chapters 1–7

Vocabulary Overview

Ten key words from this section are provided below with definitions and sentences about how the words are used in the book. Choose one of the vocabulary activity sheets (pages 15 or 16) for students to complete as they read this section. Monitor students as they work to ensure the definitions they have found are accurate and relate to the text. Finally, discuss these important vocabulary words with students. If you think these words or other words in the section warrant more time devoted to them, there are suggestions in the introduction for other vocabulary activities (page 5).

Word	Definition	Sentence about Text
tinder (ch. 1)	dry material such as grass or wood used to start a fire	Xing Xing feeds **tinder** to the dying fire.
grimaced (ch. 2)	twisted one's facial expression to show disgust or pain	Wei Ping **grimaces** with pain as she rubs her sore legs.
lamented (ch. 2)	expressed unhappiness about something	Stepmother **laments** the growing size of Wei Ping's feet.
profusion (ch. 3)	a large amount of something	Xing Xing sees the polliwogs swirling in **profusion** at the sides of the river.
venerable (ch. 3)	old and respected	Xing Xing calls Master Tang, "**Venerable** Elder."
rendered (ch. 5)	caused someone to be in a specific condition	The pain from Wei Ping's bound feet **renders** her a prisoner in her own home.
fervently (ch. 5)	in a strong or passionate manner	Xing Xing **fervently** hopes that Wei Ping will soon find a husband.
amenable (ch. 7)	willing to agree with something that is wanted	Stepmother hopes to find an **amenable** go-between to help Wei Ping find a husband.
steadfastly (ch. 7)	in a devoted and firm manner	Wei Ping **steadfastly** ignores her mother's question because she does not want to answer it.
stricken (ch. 7)	affected by sorrow or trouble	Stepmother looks **stricken** when Wei Ping suggests she marry again.

Name _____

Date _____

Chapters 1–7

Understanding Vocabulary Words

Directions: The following words appear in this section of the book. Use context clues and reference materials to determine an accurate definition for each word.

Word	Definition
tinder (ch. 1)	
grimaced (ch. 2)	
lamented (ch. 2)	
profusion (ch. 3)	
venerable (ch. 3)	
rendered (ch. 5)	
fervently (ch. 5)	
amenable (ch. 7)	
steadfastly (ch. 7)	
stricken (ch. 7)	

Chapters 1–7

Name _____

Date _____

During-Reading Vocabulary Activity

Directions: As you read these chapters, record at least eight important words on the lines below. Try to find interesting, difficult, intriguing, special, or funny words. Your words can be long or short. They can be hard or easy to spell. After each word, use context clues in the text and reference materials to define the word.

- _____
- _____
- _____
- _____
- _____
- _____
- _____
- _____
- _____
- _____

Directions: Respond to these questions about the words in this section.

1. Why should the size of Wei Ping's feet be **lamented**?

   _____
   _____
   _____

2. Why is Stepmother so **stricken** by the idea of marrying again?

   _____
   _____
   _____

Analyzing the Literature

Provided below are discussion questions you can use in small groups, with the whole class, or for written assignments. Each question is given at two levels so you can choose the right question for each group of students. Activity sheets with these questions are provided (pages 18–19) if you want students to write their responses. For each question, a few key discussion points are provided for your reference.

Story Element	■ Level 1	▲ Level 2	Key Discussion Points
Plot	What types of superstitions do you notice in the text?	What superstitions does Xing Xing's family believe? Why might they believe in them?	Stepmother refuses to fix a squeaky door because the noise keeps away demons, and the picture of the characters "fine beauty" and "great wealth" invite luck. The family might believe the superstitions because they have heard them their whole lives. The superstitions might make them feel like they can have control of their lives.
Character	How does Xing Xing treat her family? Use examples from the text.	What do Xing Xing's actions toward her family show about her character? Use examples from the text.	Xing Xing treats her family with kindness and respect even though they do not treat her the same. She hurries to get Wei Ping food because she does not want her to have any discomfort. She forgives Wei Ping's hateful words because she knows her feet hurt. She brings the carp home for Wei Ping's amusement.
Setting	Describe the setting of the story (time and place).	How might the story be different if it were set in another time or place?	The story is set in China (during the Ming Dynasty, sometime between 1300 and 1600). If it were set in another place or time, foot binding might not happen at all. Xing Xing might be able to have a life and find a husband with Stepmother's help.
Character	What was unusual about Mother's deathbed wish to Xing Xing?	How did Mother's deathbed wish affect Stepmother's relationships with Xing Xing and Wei Ping?	Mother asked Xing Xing to serve her father like a wife by making his meals and washing his feet. It makes Stepmother resent Xing Xing, but it helps her grow closer to and appreciate her daughter, Wei Ping.

Chapters 1–7

Name _____

Date _____

Analyzing the Literature

Directions: Think about the section you just read. Read each question, and state your response with textual evidence.

1. What types of superstitions do you notice in the text?

   _____
   _____
   _____
   _____

2. How does Xing Xing treat her family? Give examples from the story.

   _____
   _____
   _____
   _____
   _____

3. Describe the setting of the story (time and place).

   _____
   _____
   _____
   _____

4. What was unusual about Mother's deathbed wish to Xing Xing?

   _____
   _____
   _____
   _____
   _____

Name _____

Date _____

Chapters 1–7

▲ Analyzing the Literature

Directions: Think about the section you just read. Read each question, and state your response with textual evidence.

1. What superstitions does Xing Xing's family believe? Why might they believe in them?

   _____
   _____
   _____
   _____

2. What do Xing Xing's actions toward her family show about her character? Give examples from the story.

   _____
   _____
   _____
   _____

3. How might the story be different if it were set in another time or place?

   _____
   _____
   _____
   _____

4. How did Mother's deathbed wish affect Stepmother's relationships with Xing Xing and Wei Ping?

   _____
   _____
   _____
   _____

Chapters 1–7

Name _____

Date _____

Reader Response

Directions: Choose one of the following prompts about this section to answer. Be sure you include a topic sentence in your response, use textual evidence to support your opinion, and provide a strong conclusion that summarizes your opinion.

Writing Prompts

- **Opinion/Argument Piece**—While out hunting, Xing Xing kills the two blind raccoon kits. What would you have done if you were in her place?
- **Narrative Piece**—The carp swims into Xing Xing's pail three times before she decides to bring it home. What role might the fish play in the story?

_____
_____
_____
_____
_____
_____
_____
_____
_____
_____
_____
_____
_____
_____
_____
_____
_____

Name _____

Date _____

Chapters 1–7

Close Reading the Literature

Directions: Closely reread the section in chapter 2 about Xing Xing's father. Begin with, "Xing Xing's mother had died." Continue until, "the woman swore that with the proper binding, they would shrink." Read each question, and then revisit the text to find evidence that supports your answer.

1. Why does the author include this flashback in the book? Use the text to explain its importance.

   _____
   _____
   _____
   _____

2. According to the text, why did Father not want to hire a slave girl to help him with his pottery?

   _____
   _____
   _____
   _____

3. How does this text influence your feelings about Stepmother? Give support from the passage.

   _____
   _____
   _____
   _____

4. Use the text to describe why Father did not care about tradition.

   _____
   _____
   _____
   _____

Chapters 1–7

Name _____

Date _____

Making Connections–Lotus Feet

Directions: Read the information in the text box, and look at the picture. Then, answer the questions.

Bound feet were fashionable in China for over 1,000 years. Men thought it was beautiful, so it helped a woman find a husband. Binding began when a girl was only five or six years old. Her big toe was left alone, but her other toes were broken and bent down to the bottom of her foot. Then, both feet would be wrapped very tightly. Bandages were changed several times a week. Each time, the bandages were wrapped more tightly to make the foot smaller. The ball of the foot was brought closer to the heel. The ideal foot was only four inches long. Foot binding is no longer done in China.

1. Why would women bind the feet of their young daughters?

   _____

   _____

2. How was the foot made smaller?

   _____

   _____

   _____

3. What other practices can you think of where people change their bodies with the hope of looking more attractive?

   _____

   _____

   _____

Name _____

Date _____

Chapters 1–7

Creating with the Story Elements

Directions: Thinking about the story elements of character, setting, and plot in a novel is very important to understanding what is happening and why. Complete **one** of the following activities based on what you've read so far. Be creative and have fun!

Characters
Make a small family tree showing how Xing Xing, her parents, Stepmother, and Wei Ping are related to each other.

Setting
Create a drawing of what Xing Xing's home might look like. Include the beds, fire, *kang*, and any other details included in chapters 1–7.

Plot
Xing Xing has a gift for writing in calligraphy, one of the three perfections. Find an example of a calligraphy font, and use it to copy a poem from the book. Master Tam's poem is in chapter 3 and Xing Xing's is in chapter 5.

© Shell Education — 51769—Instructional Guide: Bound

Section 2
Chapters 8–13

Vocabulary Overview

Ten key words from this section are provided below with definitions and sentences about how the words are used in the book. Choose one of the vocabulary activity sheets (pages 25 or 26) for students to complete as they read this section. Monitor students as they work to ensure the definitions they have found are accurate and relate to the text. Finally, discuss these important vocabulary words with students. If you think these words or other words in the section warrant more time devoted to them, there are suggestions in the introduction for other vocabulary activities (page 5).

Word	Definition	Sentence about Text
wrested (ch. 8)	pulled something away by force	Xing Xing **wrests** the unripe dates from their stems.
affinity (ch. 9)	a liking for something	Xing Xing feels an **affinity** to the *yang* rather than the *yin*.
evoked (ch. 9)	brought to mind	Xing Xing's name **evokes** a sense of brightness.
incessant (ch. 9)	continuing without stopping	Frogs cannot survive the Yangzi River because of its **incessant** winds.
shards (ch. 10)	sharp pieces of broken ceramic or glass	Mei Zing shows Xing Xing **shards** of pottery.
shrine (ch. 11)	a place people visit that is connected to a special place or person	Stepmother, Xing Xing, and Wei Ping gather at the family **shrine**.
invocation (ch. 11)	the act of asking for help or support from something	Xing Xing listens carefully to Stepmother's **invocation**.
naïve (ch. 11)	showing a lack of experience or knowledge	It is **naïve** to believe spirits cannot be anywhere at any time.
optimism (ch. 12)	a belief that good things will happen in the future	Xing Xing approaches the shopkeeper with **optimism** when looking for the *lang zhong*.
askew (ch. 13)	not straight; crooked	Xing Xing knocks a cart full of birds **askew** when climbing into the cart.

Name _____

Date _____

Chapters 8–13

Understanding Vocabulary Words

Directions: The following words appear in this section of the book. Use context clues and reference materials to determine an accurate definition for each word.

Word	Definition
wrested (ch. 8)	
affinity (ch. 9)	
evoked (ch. 9)	
incessant (ch. 9)	
shards (ch. 10)	
shrine (ch. 11)	
invocation (ch. 11)	
naïve (ch. 11)	
optimism (ch. 12)	
askew (ch. 13)	

Chapters 8–13

Name _____

Date _____

During-Reading Vocabulary Activity

Directions: As you read these chapters, record at least eight important words on the lines below. Try to find interesting, difficult, intriguing, special, or funny words. Your words can be long or short. They can be hard or easy to spell. After each word, use context clues in the text and reference materials to define the word.

- _____
- _____
- _____
- _____
- _____
- _____
- _____
- _____
- _____
- _____

Directions: Respond to these questions about the words in this section.

1. What makes the **shard** of pottery special?
   _____
   _____
   _____

2. Why do Xing Xing, Stepmother, and Wei Ping visit the family **shrine**?
   _____
   _____
   _____
   _____

Section 2
Chapters 8–13

Analyzing the Literature

Provided below are discussion questions you can use in small groups, with the whole class, or for written assignments. Each question is given at two levels so you can choose the right question for each group of students. Activity sheets with these questions are provided (pages 28–29) if you want students to write their responses. For each question, a few key discussion points are provided for your reference.

Story Element	■ Level 1	▲ Level 2	Key Discussion Points
Character	What actions does Stepmother carry out at Father's grave?	Describe Stepmother's actions at Father's grave, and explain why she does them.	Stepmother burns incense to invite ghosts and spirits. She promises to raise Wei Ping's second son as Father's male heir to please him. She calls Xing Xing by her real name to make Father's spirit think his daughter is being treated well. She burns money to show reverence for the Wu ancestors.
Character	Why does Xing Xing not have many friends?	How does Xing Xing's education affect her relationships with girls her own age?	Xing Xing has an education and can read and write. This makes many girls uncomfortable because she is unlike the others. The other girls do not know how to respond to her education and do not trust her, so Xing Xing does not interact with them.
Setting	Why must Xing Xing travel to a different village?	How might Xing Xing's travel to a different village affect the story?	The *lang zhong* has already left their village, and Xing Xing must give him unripe dates he can use in medicine. Her travel might introduce new characters, it might create a problem or solution, or it might make Xing Xing learn something about herself or others.
Plot	Describe Xing Xing's interactions with the cart driver.	What do Xing Xing's interactions with the cart driver show about her culture?	The cart driver offers her a ride to the village, but he seems to be taking a different route when it becomes dark. She becomes suspicious and secretly jumps off the cart. He tries to find her. This shows women (and girls) are expected to believe and obey men. Their personal safety can be in danger.

Chapters 8–13

Name _____

Date _____

Analyzing the Literature

Directions: Think about the section you just read. Read each question, and state your response with textual evidence.

1. What actions does Stepmother carry out at Father's grave?

   _____
   _____
   _____
   _____
   _____

2. Why does Xing Xing not have many friends?

   _____
   _____
   _____
   _____
   _____

3. Why must Xing Xing travel to a different village?

   _____
   _____
   _____
   _____
   _____

4. Describe Xing Xing's interactions with the cart driver.

   _____
   _____
   _____
   _____
   _____

Name _____

Date _____

Chapters 8–13

▲ Analyzing the Literature

Directions: Think about the section you just read. Read each question, and state your response with textual evidence.

1. Describe Stepmother's actions at Father's grave, and explain why she does them.

   _____
   _____
   _____
   _____
   _____

2. How does Xing Xing's education affect her relationships with girls her own age?

   _____
   _____
   _____
   _____

3. How might Xing Xing's travel to a different village affect the story?

   _____
   _____
   _____
   _____
   _____

4. What do Xing Xing's interactions with the cart driver show about her culture?

   _____
   _____
   _____
   _____
   _____

© Shell Education

Chapters 8–13

Name _____

Date _____

Reader Response

Directions: Choose one of the following prompts about this section to answer. Be sure you include a topic sentence in your response, use textual evidence to support your opinion, and provide a strong conclusion that summarizes your opinion.

Writing Prompts

- **Narrative Piece**—The text briefly explains the concept of *yin* and *yang*. Xing Xing relates more to the *yang*. Which do you relate to? Explain your reasoning.
- **Informative/Explanatory Piece**—What questions do you have about Xing Xing's fish? Write at least two, and make predictions about what you think the answers might be.

_____
_____
_____
_____
_____
_____
_____
_____
_____
_____
_____
_____
_____
_____
_____
_____
_____
_____

Name _____

Date _____

Chapters 8–13

Close Reading the Literature

Directions: Closely reread the section in chapter 8 after the raccoon attacks Wei Ping. Begin with, "Stepmother washed Wei Ping's feet." Stop at the end of the chapter. Read each question, and then revisit the text to find evidence that supports your answer.

1. What does the author want readers to infer from this passage? Use text evidence to support your answer.

   _____
   _____
   _____
   _____

2. Use examples from the text to describe the different emotions Stepmother feels in the passage.

   _____
   _____
   _____
   _____

3. What do Wei Ping's actions show about her in this section? Give support from the text.

   _____
   _____
   _____
   _____

4. According to Stepmother, why did the raccoon attack Wei Ping?

   _____
   _____
   _____

Chapters 8–13

Name _____

Date _____

Making Connections–Old Sayings

Directions: Stepmother quotes an old saying to Wei Ping after the raccoon attack. Match that saying and the others to their meanings.

1. The eagle swoops down when the hare stirs. _____

2. A stitch in time saves nine. _____

3. Slow and steady wins the race. _____

4. Well begun is half done. _____

5. You can catch more flies with honey than with vinegar. _____

A. Trying to finish something quickly is not the best way to accomplish a task.

B. A person must act quickly to take advantage of a good situation.

C. Using kind words will help a person more than being harsh.

D. Taking care of a small problem right away is much easier than waiting until it turns into a big problem.

E. Getting a good start to a project means a lot of the work is already finished.

Name _____

Date _____

Chapters 8–13

Creating with the Story Elements

Directions: Thinking about the story elements of character, setting, and plot in a novel is very important to understanding what is happening and why. Complete **one** of the following activities based on what you've read so far. Be creative and have fun!

Characters

Create a T-chart about Stepmother. Write good characteristics about her on one side and bad on the other.

Setting

Xing Xing enjoys her time with the slave boy as they ride the cart to the next village. Write a poem describing what they do and see on the way.

Plot

Draw a picture of Xing Xing's beautiful fish. Use descriptions from the text to help.

Section 3 Chapters 14–17

Vocabulary Overview

Ten key words from this section are provided below with definitions and sentences about how the words are used in the book. Choose one of the vocabulary activity sheets (pages 35 or 36) for students to complete as they read this section. Monitor students as they work to ensure the definitions they have found are accurate and relate to the text. Finally, discuss these important vocabulary words with students. If you think these words or other words in the section warrant more time devoted to them, there are suggestions in the introduction for other vocabulary activities (page 5).

Word	Definition	Sentence about Text
litany (ch. 14)	a prayer where the people repeat the words of the leader	Xing Xing repeats a silent **litany** to herself in her head.
sidled (ch. 14)	moved close to something in a quiet, sneaky way	Xing Xing **sidles** along the edge of the water until she comes to another bramble.
alighted (ch. 14)	stopped on a surface after flying	A bird **alights** on a boulder in mid-stream.
benevolent (ch. 14)	kind and generous	Xing Xing comes to a temple with statues of **benevolent** dragons on its roof.
elixir (ch. 14)	a magical liquid that can cure an illness	The patient gets a refill of the **elixir** he needs and leaves.
alchemy (ch. 15)	a power that changes something in a mysterious way	Yao Wang uses **alchemy** to help others live a long life.
efficacy (ch. 15)	the power to make a result that is wanted	Yao Wang uses acupuncture to its greatest **efficacy**.
charlatans (ch. 16)	people who pretend to know something in order to deceive others	The pharmacist wants to know how he can conduct business when **charlatans** sell their junk in the street.
culpable (ch. 16)	guilty of doing something wrong	Yao Wang is **culpable** because the letters are not under the glaze.
scribe (ch. 17)	a person with the job of copying a book or message	Yao Wang tells the boat captain that Xing Xing is a talented **scribe**.

Name _____

Date _____

Chapters 14–17

Understanding Vocabulary Words

Directions: The following words appear in this section of the book. Use context clues and reference materials to determine an accurate definition for each word.

Word	Definition
litany (ch. 14)	
sidled (ch. 14)	
alighted (ch. 14)	
benevolent (ch. 14)	
elixir (ch. 14)	
alchemy (ch. 15)	
efficacy (ch. 15)	
charlatans (ch. 16)	
culpable (ch. 16)	
scribe (ch. 17)	

Chapters 14–17

Name _____

Date _____

During-Reading Vocabulary Activity

Directions: As you read these chapters, record at least eight important words on the lines below. Try to find interesting, difficult, intriguing, special, or funny words. Your words can be long or short. They can be hard or easy to spell. After each word, use context clues in the text and reference materials to define the word.

- _____
- _____
- _____
- _____
- _____
- _____
- _____
- _____
- _____
- _____

Directions: Now, organize your words. Rewrite each of your words on a sticky note. Work as a group to create a bar graph of your words. You should stack any words that are the same on top of one another. Different words appear in different columns. Finally, discuss with a group why certain words were chosen more often than other words.

Analyzing the Literature

Provided below are discussion questions you can use in small groups, with the whole class, or for written assignments. Each question is given at two levels so you can choose the right question for each group of students. Activity sheets with these questions are provided (pages 38–39) if you want students to write their responses. For each question, a few key discussion points are provided for your reference.

Story Element	■ Level 1	▲ Level 2	Key Discussion Points
Plot	Why is Xing Xing so surprised to see the beautiful fish after she escapes from the cart driver?	After her escape from the cart driver, why does Xing Xing feel both happy and concerned to see the beautiful fish?	Xing Xing is far from home, and the water she is walking in does not feed into where the fish lives at her home. She loves the fish and finds comfort in her, but she is concerned because she does not know how the fish will be able to swim upstream. She also knows if a fisherman sees the fish, he will want to catch her.
Character	Why does Yao Wang refuse to let Xing Xing tell her story when they first meet?	When Yao Wang will not let Xing Xing tell her story at first, what does it show about his character?	Yao Wang says she needs food, rest, and time before she can tell her whole story to him. This shows he is wise because he can sense she has a lot to say. He is willing to be patient to hear the entire truth.
Character	How does Yao Wang eventually agree to help Wei Ping?	Though Yao Wang agrees to help Wei Ping, why is Xing Xing still concerned?	Yao Wang will not travel to their village, but he sends Xing Xing with a bag of medicine to Wei Ping. Xing Xing is worried she will not apply it correctly and do more damage. She is also worried Yao Wang might really be a charlatan and the medicine won't work.
Setting	What new experiences does Xing Xing have traveling by boat?	How might traveling by boat be a good change for Xing Xing?	Xing Xing does not know how to swim, so she must fight her fear of drowning. She enjoys breathing the smell of the wet river water. While spending time with the captain, she has fun making faces at herself in the mirror, and she begins to broaden her thinking by wondering if anyone knows what true madness is.

Chapters 14–17

Name _____

Date _____

Analyzing the Literature

Directions: Think about the section you just read. Read each question, and state your response with textual evidence.

1. Why is Xing Xing so surprised to see the beautiful fish after she escapes from the cart driver?

   _____
   _____
   _____
   _____

2. Why does Yao Wang refuse to let Xing Xing tell her story when they first meet?

   _____
   _____
   _____
   _____

3. How does Yao Wang eventually agree to help Wei Ping?

   _____
   _____
   _____
   _____

4. What new experiences does Xing Xing have traveling by boat?

   _____
   _____
   _____
   _____

Name _____

Date _____

Chapters 14–17

▲ Analyzing the Literature

Directions: Think about the section you just read. Read each question, and state your response with textual evidence.

1. After her escape from the cart driver, why does Xing Xing feel both happy and concerned to see the beautiful fish?

   _____
   _____
   _____
   _____

2. When Yao Wang will not let Xing Xing tell her story at first, what does it show about his character?

   _____
   _____
   _____
   _____

3. Though Yao Wang agrees to help Wei Ping, why is Xing Xing still concerned?

   _____
   _____
   _____
   _____

4. How might traveling by boat be a good change for Xing Xing?

   _____
   _____
   _____
   _____
   _____

Chapters 14–17

Name _____

Date _____

Reader Response

Directions: Choose one of the following prompts about this section to answer. Be sure you include a topic sentence in your response, use textual evidence to support your opinion, and provide a strong conclusion that summarizes your opinion.

Writing Prompts

- **Narrative Piece**—When Xing Xing arrives in the village, she sees new people and foods, animals, the temple in the town's center, and even a restaurant. Write about a time you went somewhere new. What did you see and experience?
- **Opinion/Argument Piece**—Do you think Xing Xing should have told Yao Wang her entire story? Use the text or examples from your own life to support your opinion.

_____
_____
_____
_____
_____
_____
_____
_____
_____
_____
_____
_____
_____
_____
_____

Name _____

Date _____

Close Reading the Literature

Chapters 14–17

Directions: Closely reread the confrontation between Yao Wang and the official in chapter 16. Begin when Xing Xing says, "It's my fault, not Yao Wang's." Continue until the official says, "his daughter talks just like you or me." Read each question, and then revisit the text to find evidence that supports your answer.

1. Yao Wang says, "Kong Fu Zi says that lack of talent in a woman is a virtue." Use textual evidence to show the officials believe this.

   _____
   _____
   _____
   _____

2. Do you think Yao Wang believes his statement about Kong Fu Zi? Use the text to support your opinion.

   _____
   _____
   _____
   _____

3. Based on the text, what does Xing Xing think of Yao Wang's statement about Kong Fu Zi?

   _____
   _____
   _____

4. Use examples from the passage to describe the ideas of the new emperor.

   _____
   _____
   _____

Chapters 14–17

Name _____

Date _____

Making Connections—Home Remedies

Directions: Yao Wang is a *lang zhong*. This means he is not a true doctor but can still help people get well. Today, many people use home remedies. Interview at least two adults, and find out how they would treat these common health problems without going to the doctor or taking medicine.

Health Problem	Home Remedy
headache	
sore throat	
twisted ankle	
burn	
can't sleep	

Name _____

Date _____

Chapters 14–17

Creating with the Story Elements

Directions: Thinking about the story elements of character, setting, and plot in a novel is very important to understanding what is happening and why. Complete **one** of the following activities based on what you've read so far. Be creative and have fun!

Characters

Xing Xing has spent time with Stepmother and Yao Wang. Create a Venn diagram comparing and contrasting her interactions with both.

Setting

Write a letter from Xing Xing to Wei Ping describing the village she visited and the boat she rode on during her trip to find Yao Wang.

Plot

Create a time line of the different events that happen from when Xing Xing arrives in the village to when she leaves it. Include at least six events in your time line.

Section 4
Chapters 18–23

Teacher Plans

Vocabulary Overview

Ten key words from this section are provided below with definitions and sentences about how the words are used in the book. Choose one of the vocabulary activity sheets (pages 45 or 46) for students to complete as they read this section. Monitor students as they work to ensure the definitions they have found are accurate and relate to the text. Finally, discuss these important vocabulary words with students. If you think these words or other words in the section warrant more time devoted to them, there are suggestions in the introduction for other vocabulary activities (page 5).

Word	Definition	Sentence about Text
ominous (ch. 18)	suggesting that something bad is going to happen	The blowing wind on the water feels **ominous**.
demented (ch. 18)	unable to determine what is real and what is not; insane	Stepmother and Wei Ping seem **demented** when Xing Xing returns to the cave.
discreetly (ch. 18)	doing something carefully so it will not cause embarrassment	Xing Xing tries to **discreetly** change the clothes of Stepmother and Wei Ping.
reincarnation (ch. 18)	the rebirth of a soul into a new body	The beautiful fish is the **reincarnation** of Xing Xing's mother.
manipulating (ch. 19)	influencing a person in an unfair way	Wei Ping is **manipulating** Xing Xing by calling her "sister."
mediate (ch. 20)	to work with arguing sides in order to find a peaceful agreement	China's emperor can **mediate** between heaven and earth.
dissociated (ch. 21)	separated or disconnected	Xing Xing enters the cave feeling **dissociated** from her body.
prostrate (ch. 22)	lying flat on the ground with one's face downward	Xing Xing lays **prostrate** in the field, crying about the beautiful fish.
demurely (ch. 23)	doing something in a shy or modest way	Xing Xing drinks the potion from Stepmother and lowers her eyes **demurely**.
pinnacle (ch. 23)	the highest point of something; a mountaintop	Xing Xing's mind jumps from one **pinnacle** to another even though her body is slow from the potion.

Name _____

Date _____

Understanding Vocabulary Words

Chapters 18–23

Directions: The following words appear in this section of the book. Use context clues and reference materials to determine an accurate definition for each word.

Word	Definition
ominous (ch. 18)	
demented (ch. 18)	
discreetly (ch. 18)	
reincarnation (ch. 18)	
manipulating (ch. 19)	
mediate (ch. 20)	
dissociated (ch. 21)	
prostrate (ch. 22)	
demurely (ch. 23)	
pinnacle (ch. 23)	

Chapters 18–23

Name _____

Date _____

During-Reading Vocabulary Activity

Directions: As you read these chapters, record at least eight important words on the lines below. Try to find interesting, difficult, intriguing, special, or funny words. Your words can be long or short. They can be hard or easy to spell. After each word, use context clues in the text and reference materials to define the word.

- _____
- _____
- _____
- _____
- _____
- _____
- _____
- _____
- _____
- _____

Directions: Respond to these questions about the words in this section.

1. Why does Xing Xing think the beautiful fish is the **reincarnation** of her mother?

   _____
   _____
   _____
   _____

2. Why does Xing Xing feel **dissociated** from her body?

   _____
   _____
   _____

Analyzing the Literature

Provided below are discussion questions you can use in small groups, with the whole class, or for written assignments. Each question is given at two levels so you can choose the right question for each group of students. Activity sheets with these questions are provided (pages 48–49) if you want students to write their responses. For each question, a few key discussion points are provided for your reference.

Story Element	■ Level 1	▲ Level 2	Key Discussion Points
Setting	Describe the cave home when Xing Xing returns from her journey.	What is wrong when Xing Xing returns to the cave home? Why is it like this?	The cave home is filthy and smelly. It has not been cleaned, the fire has gone out, there are piles of animal bones and pits, and the chamber pot has overflowed. While Xing Xing was gone, Stepmother and Wei Ping were afraid a demon would come, so they did nothing but huddle together on the *kang*.
Character	How does Stepmother show she is interested in the beautiful fish?	Why is Stepmother so interested in seeing the beautiful fish?	Stepmother asks questions about the fish and even makes the difficult walk to the pool to try and see her. She wants to see the fish because she is suspicious about what it might be. Xing Xing feeds the fish with her *shizhi*, and the fish comes up to the bank to see her.
Plot	Why does Xing Xing become concerned about her fish mother when she is at Master Tang's home?	What clues does Xing Xing notice that help her figure out what happened to her fish mother?	At Master Tang's, she learns that Stepmother has given away large amounts of fish. Also, the fish in the stew is cut up very small as if to hide it, and Xing Xing's dress is wet when she returns from Master Tang's.
Plot	Why is Xing Xing suspicious when Stepmother offers to empty the chamber pot?	What is the significance of Stepmother offering to empty the chamber pot?	Stepmother's most hated chore is to empty the chamber pot. When she offers to take care of it, Xing Xing knows Stepmother is trying to keep her away from the dung heap. This gives Xing Xing a clue to find out what happened to her fish mother.

Chapters 18–23

Name _____

Date _____

Analyzing the Literature

Directions: Think about the section you just read. Read each question, and state your response with textual evidence.

1. Describe the cave home when Xing Xing returns from her journey.

   _____
   _____
   _____
   _____

2. How does Stepmother show she is interested in the beautiful fish?

   _____
   _____
   _____
   _____

3. Why does Xing Xing become concerned about her fish mother when she is at Master Tang's home?

   _____
   _____
   _____
   _____

4. Why is Xing Xing suspicious when Stepmother offers to empty the chamber pot?

   _____
   _____
   _____
   _____
   _____

Name _____

Date _____

▲ Analyzing the Literature

Chapters 18–23

Directions: Think about the section you just read. Read each question, and state your response with textual evidence.

1. What is wrong when Xing Xing returns to the cave home? Why is it like this?

   _____
   _____
   _____
   _____

2. Why is Stepmother so interested in seeing the beautiful fish?

   _____
   _____
   _____
   _____

3. What clues does Xing Xing notice that help her figure out what happened to her fish mother?

   _____
   _____
   _____
   _____

4. What is the significance of Stepmother offering to empty the chamber pot?

   _____
   _____
   _____
   _____

Chapters 18–23

Name _____

Date _____

Reader Response

Directions: Choose one of the following prompts about this section to answer. Be sure you include a topic sentence in your response, use textual evidence to support your opinion, and provide a strong conclusion that summarizes your opinion.

Writing Prompts

- **Opinion/Argument Piece**—Xing Xing believes the spirit of her mother has been reincarnated as the beautiful fish. Do you believe this is possible? Why or why not?
- **Informatory/Explanatory Piece**—Xing Xing keeps her suspicions about what Stepmother has done to her mother fish from Wei Ping. Why does she do this? What does it show about the characters of Xing Xing and Wei Ping?

_____
_____
_____
_____
_____
_____
_____
_____
_____
_____
_____
_____
_____
_____

Name _____

Date _____

Chapters 18–23

Close Reading the Literature

Directions: Closely reread Xing Xing's confrontation with Stepmother in chapter 22. Begin with, "She had run far; it took a long time to walk home." Continue reading until the end of the chapter. Read each question, and then revisit the text to find evidence that supports your answer.

1. How does Xing Xing think her dress got wet? Use inferencing based on the text to explain your answer.

   _____
   _____
   _____

2. According to the passage, why does Xing Xing want to tell Wei Ping what Stepmother did?

   _____
   _____
   _____

3. How does Xing Xing show she is growing more confident in this passage? Support your answer with references from the text.

   _____
   _____
   _____
   _____

4. Xing Xing feels Stepmother did not give a confession. Do you think she did? Use the dialogue in the text to defend your opinion.

   _____
   _____
   _____
   _____

Chapters 18–23

Name _____

Date _____

Making Connections–Compose a *Ci*

Directions: Xing Xing composes a six-line poem called a *ci* to share at the cave celebration. Her *ci* has a rhyming pattern of AA, BB, CC. Write your own *ci* below. Some ideas are given in the text box, or you can choose your own topic. Then, draw a picture to go with your *ci*.

Word Bank		
sports	animals	school
hobbies	food	neighborhood
nature	friends	family

_____
_____
_____
_____
_____
_____

Name _____

Date _____

Chapters 18–23

Creating with the Story Elements

Directions: Thinking about the story elements of character, setting, and plot in a novel is very important to understanding what is happening and why. Complete **one** of the following activities based on what you've read so far. Be creative and have fun!

Characters

The beautiful fish is very important to Xing Xing. Make a graphic organizer using events in the book that show how the beautiful fish is different from a regular fish.

Setting

Readers do not know what it was like in the cave for Stepmother and Wei Ping while Xing Xing was away. Use information given in the text to write about what might have happened.

Plot

Imagine you are a detective investigating the disappearance of the beautiful fish. Make a list of characters you would need to talk to and questions you would ask them.

Section 5
Chapters 24–29

Vocabulary Overview

Ten key words from this section are provided below with definitions and sentences about how the words are used in the book. Choose one of the vocabulary activity sheets (pages 55 or 56) for students to complete as they read this section. Monitor students as they work to ensure the definitions they have found are accurate and relate to the text. Finally, discuss these important vocabulary words with students. If you think these words or other words in the section warrant more time devoted to them, there are suggestions in the introduction for other vocabulary activities (page 5).

Word	Definition	Sentence about Text
reverence (ch. 24)	deep respect for a person or thing	Xing Xing needs to show **reverence** to her fish mother's bones.
feigning (ch. 25)	pretending to feel or be affected by something	Xing Xing begins **feigning** pain so she does not have to go to the festival with her family.
exude (ch. 25)	to show a quality very strongly	The golden shoes **exude** grace.
corpulent (ch. 26)	fat; large and bulky	Most of the men at the cave celebration are **corpulent**.
inevitable (ch. 26)	certain to happen	Xing Xing waits for the **inevitable** screaming of Stepmother.
pungent (ch. 27)	having a strong taste or smell	The figs create a **pungent** sweetness in the air.
sham (ch. 28)	something that is not what it appears to be in order to trick someone	Xing Xing feels a stolen poem is a **sham** compared to everything else that has happened to her.
subservient (ch. 29)	very willing to obey someone else	The prince tells Xing Xing she is not **subservient**.
impertinent (ch. 29)	rude or not showing the proper respect	Xing Xing feels being called **impertinent** by the prince is charming.
pertinent (ch. 29)	clearly related and important to a topic	The prince wonders if Xing Xing is actually the **pertinent** one.

Name

Date

Chapters 24–29

Understanding Vocabulary Words

Directions: The following words appear in this section of the book. Use context clues and reference materials to determine an accurate definition for each word.

Word	Definition
reverence (ch. 24)	
feigning (ch. 25)	
exude (ch. 25)	
corpulent (ch. 26)	
inevitable (ch. 26)	
pungent (ch. 27)	
sham (ch. 28)	
subservient (ch. 29)	
impertinent (ch. 29)	
pertinent (ch. 29)	

Chapters 24–29

Name _____

Date _____

During-Reading Vocabulary Activity

Directions: As you read these chapters, choose five important words from the story. Then, use those five words to complete this word flow chart. On each arrow, write a vocabulary word. In the boxes between the words, explain how the words connect. An example for the words *subservient* and *impertinent* has been done for you.

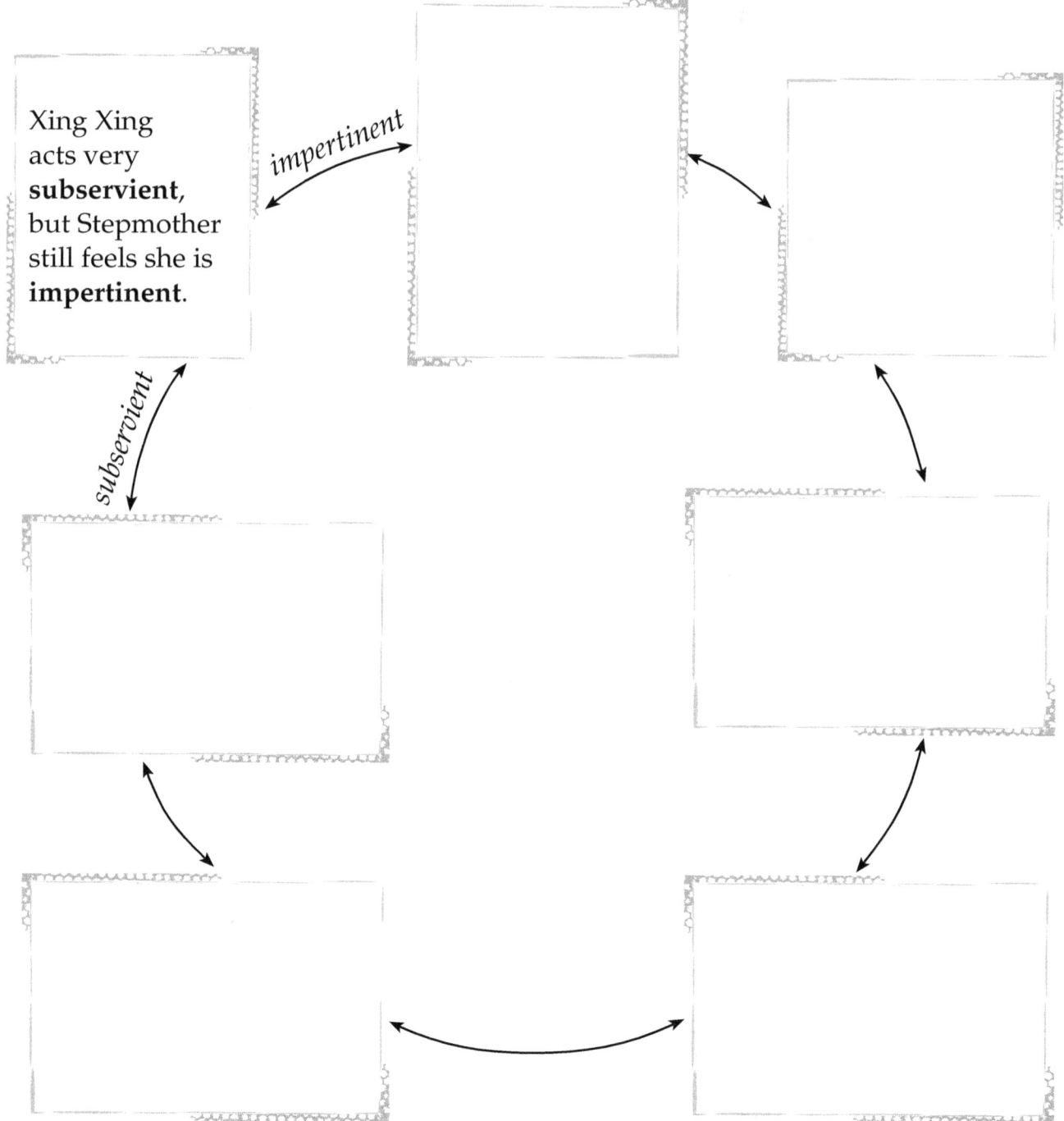

Analyzing the Literature

Provided below are discussion questions you can use in small groups, with the whole class, or for written assignments. Each question is given at two levels so you can choose the right question for each group of students. Activity sheets with these questions are provided (pages 58–59) if you want students to write their responses. For each question, a few key discussion points are provided for your reference.

Story Element	■ Level 1	▲ Level 2	Key Discussion Points
Plot	Why did Xing Xing's mother want her to serve her father and be at his deathbed?	Why does Stepmother say Xing Xing had been married to her father?	Xing Xing's mother wanted her there so Father could tell her about the letter and gifts. Xing Xing served her father and washed his feet when he was still alive, and her mother asked her to be at his side when he died. All of these are a wife's duty.
Character	What does Xing Xing's mother tell her she can do with the gifts?	How does Xing Xing's mother's letter show she is understanding?	Her mother tells Xing Xing she should do what makes sense with the gifts. She can add them to her treasures or sell them or use them to make herself beautiful. Her mother realizes Xing Xing may have different needs depending on the direction of her life.
Setting	What special things does Xing Xing experience at the cave festival?	How do the special things Xing Xing experiences at the cave festival make her yearn for more?	Xing Xing tastes new, foreign foods, and she sees birds from different places. They make her think about places outside her little village. She wants to see what is beyond the Great Wall and in the South China Sea.
Plot	How does the prince show Xing Xing he likes her as she is?	How does the conversation between Xing Xing and the prince show they will be a good match?	He lets her share about herself and is accepting about the things that others might see as a negative (her feet are not bound, she can read and write, she has no dowry). They have a playful exchange, and he uses puns, which shows he is clever.

Chapters 24–29

Name _____

Date _____

Analyzing the Literature

Directions: Think about the section you just read. Read each question, and state your response with textual evidence.

1. Why did Xing Xing's mother want her to serve her father and be at his deathbed?

   _____
   _____
   _____
   _____
   _____

2. What does Xing Xing's mother tell her she can do with the gifts?

   _____
   _____
   _____
   _____

3. What special things does Xing Xing experience at the cave festival?

   _____
   _____
   _____
   _____
   _____

4. How does the prince show Xing Xing he likes her as she is?

   _____
   _____
   _____
   _____

Name _____

Date _____

▲ Analyzing the Literature

Chapters 24–29

Directions: Think about the section you just read. Read each question, and state your response with textual evidence.

1. Why did Stepmother say Xing Xing had been married to her father?

   _____
   _____
   _____
   _____
   _____

2. How does Xing Xing's mother's letter show she is understanding?

   _____
   _____
   _____
   _____

3. How do the special things Xing Xing experiences at the cave festival make her yearn for more?

   _____
   _____
   _____
   _____
   _____

4. How does the conversation between Xing Xing and the prince show they will be a good match?

   _____
   _____
   _____
   _____

Chapters 24–29

Name _____

Date _____

Reader Response

Directions: Choose one of the following prompts about this section to answer. Be sure you include a topic sentence in your response, use textual evidence to support your opinion, and provide a strong conclusion that summarizes your opinion.

Writing Prompts

- **Informative/Explanatory Piece**—Xing Xing tries to honor the spirits of both her parents. In what ways can you honor your family members?
- **Narrative Piece**—The ending of the book comes quickly, with Xing Xing deciding to leave with the prince. Write about what you think happens next in the story. Does Xing Xing get her "happily ever after"?

_____
_____
_____
_____
_____
_____
_____
_____
_____
_____
_____
_____
_____
_____
_____
_____

Name _____

Date _____

Chapters 24–29

Close Reading the Literature

Directions: Closely reread the prince's arrival in chapter 29. Begin with, "Finally, the prince's retinue came." Continue until, "Hardly what one might expect of a prince." Read each question, and then revisit the text to find evidence that supports your answer.

1. Use information in the passage to compare and contrast how Stepmother, Wei Ping, and Xing Xing greet the prince's retinue.

   _____
   _____
   _____

2. Why does Xing Xing feel the prince's plan is a sham? Use the text to explain your answer.

   _____
   _____
   _____

3. How does Xing Xing's power grow in this passage? Use examples from the text to support your answer.

   _____
   _____
   _____
   _____

4. What evidence in the text shows the prince is not what was expected?

   _____
   _____
   _____
   _____

© Shell Education

51769—Instructional Guide: Bound **61**

Chapters 24–29

Name _____

Date _____

Making Connections–
Wanted: The Girl with the Golden Shoe

Directions: Create a poster that the prince can hang in the town to let people know of his marriage plan. Include who he is looking for, how he will find her, and what will happen when he does. Include a colorful illustration to make your poster stand out.

Name _____

Date _____

Chapters 24–29

Creating with the Story Elements

Directions: Thinking about the story elements of character, setting, and plot in a novel is very important to understanding what is happening and why. Complete **one** of the following activities based on what you've read so far. Be creative and have fun!

Characters

Xing Xing finds an important letter from her mother. Write a letter from Xing Xing to her mother's spirit, explaining how she was able to use her mother's gifts.

Setting

Both the location (China) and time (sometime between 1368 and 1644) are important to the story. Choose an alternate setting, and explain at least three ways the story would be different in a new place or time.

Plot

Stepmother and Wei Ping do not say much while Xing Xing speaks with the prince, but they must have had a lot of thoughts! Create a comic strip showing what they might have been thinking during Xing Xing's conversation.

Post-Reading Activities

Name _____

Date _____

Post-Reading Theme Thoughts

Directions: Read each of the statements in the first column. Choose a main character from *Bound*. Think about that character's point of view. From that character's perspective, decide if the character would agree or disagree with the statements. Record the character's opinion by marking an X in Agree or Disagree for each statement. Explain your choices in the fourth column using text evidence.

Character I Chose: _____

Statement	Agree	Disagree	Explain Your Answer
You should be kind to people even if they are not kind to you.			
It is okay for beauty to be painful.			
The most important thing is to take care of your family.			
Family members who have died can still be with you.			

Name _____

Date _____

Post-Reading Activities

Culminating Activity: One Story, Many Cinerellas

Overview: The fairy tale Cinderella is one of the world's most-told stories. Hundreds of different versions exist from different cultures and from people's imaginative retellings. Read at least three different versions of Cinderella stories to discover what events are most-needed to be considered part of the Cinderella collection. You must choose at least one cultural version and one imaginative retelling.

Cultural Version	Imaginative Retellings
• *The Korean Cinderella* by Shirley Climo • *The Egyptian Cinderella* by Shirley Climo • *The Rough-Face Girl* by Rafe Martin • *Cendrillon: A Caribbean Cinderella* by Robert D. San Souci	• *Bigfoot Cinderrrrella* by Tony Johnston and James Warhola • *The Salmon Princess: An Alaska Cinderella Story* by Mindy Dwyer • *Cindy Ellen: A Wild Western Cinderella* by Susan Lowell • *Prince Cinders* by Babette Cole

1. What titles did you read?

   _____
   _____
   _____

2. What events do you think a story needs to be considered a version of Cinderella?

   _____
   _____
   _____
   _____
   _____
   _____
   _____

© Shell Education

Post-Reading Activities

Name _____

Date _____

Culminating Activity: One Story, Many Cinderellas (cont.)

Directions: When you have completed your thoughts about what makes up a Cinderella story, choose one type of writing described below. Then, create your own version of Cinderella. Use the space below to brainstorm your story. Finally, write a final copy on a separate sheet of paper. Be creative and have fun!

- **Story**—This is a traditional way to tell a story. It can be made with or without illustrations.
- **Graphic Novel**—Similar to a comic strip, this is made of cells with illustrations and short text. It is mostly dialogue.
- **Play**—This way of telling a story is meant to be performed, not read. There are stage directions telling the actors what to do, but the plot of the story is told through the characters' lines.

_____
_____
_____
_____
_____
_____
_____
_____
_____
_____
_____
_____
_____

Name _____

Date _____

Comprehension Assessment

Directions: Circle the letter for the best response to each question.

1. What is the meaning of the word *sham* as it is used in the book?
    A. a covering for a pillow
    B. something meant to trick people
    C. having a disrespectful manner
    D. joking around with others

2. Which detail from the book best supports your answer to question 1?
    E. "It seemed an immodest name, even for the very wisest doctor."
    F. "Stepmother sat with her arms wrapped protectively around Wei Ping."
    G. "He wanted Xing Xing to make faces in the mirror, too."
    H. "The prince was supposed to choose a wife by using a shoe. But, surely, many women's feet would fit that shoe."

3. Write the main idea of the text below in the graphic organizer.

    "Stepmother was fond of repeating the popular saying 'Better one deformed son than many daughters wise as Buddha.'"

Main Idea (question 3)

Details (question 4)	Details (question 4)

4. Choose two supporting details to add to the graphic organizer.
    A. Xing Xing knew Wei Ping's mean comments were because her feet hurt.
    B. The Kong Fu Zi teaches it is a virtue for women to have a lack of talent.
    C. Stepmother will raise Wei Ping's second son as a male heir for Xing Xing's father.
    D. Master Tang's wife compliments Xing Xing on the clever character she put on the pot.

Comprehension Assessment (cont.)

5. Which statement best expresses one of the themes of the book?
   A. The bonds of family should be kept strong.
   B. Marriage will bring honor and happiness to women.
   C. A woman can be more than what society expects.
   D. Spirits are among the living to protect them.

6. Which detail from the book provides the best evidence for your answer to number 5?
   E. "She felt strong. A strong woman in a world that tried to deny the very existence of such a thing."
   F. "You had but to call out to a spirit of a close ancestor and it would come to you if it knew where you were."
   G. "Each morning Stepmother said that a suitor was sure to come that day with an offer of marriage."
   H. "Widows of decent families do not remarry…It is a small matter to starve to death but a large matter to lose one's virtue."

7. What is the purpose of these sentences from the book? "He [Xing Xing's father] didn't like the custom [of binding feet]. Besides, he had enjoyed the assistance of his daughters in his shop—and that work required them to have full use of their feet."

   _____
   _____
   _____

8. Which other quotation from the story serves a similar purpose?
   A. "I don't think Father ever cared much about riches…He loved simple things."
   B. "Stop this pain, Father, I beg you."
   C. "You are such generous and wise ancestors that you look after even the most unworthy of us."
   D. "Xing Xing had not noticed the aura of death around Father that morning."

Name _____

Date _____

Response to Literature: Still Bound

Post-Reading Activities

Overview: Both Xing Xing and Wei Ping are bound in the novel. Xing Xing is bound to Stepmother. Because Xing Xing is a girl, she is bound because of her inability to create her own future. Wei Ping is bound in a physical way. She tries to alter her body to become more attractive and make her feet smaller. Similar to the book, social and physical binding has happened in the United States. Here are just a few examples:

- social—slavery, right to vote, gender wage gap
- physical—corsets, orthodontics, plastic surgery

Directions: Select one way Americans have been bound socially and one way they have been bound physically. Your choices do not have to be from the list above. Do research on your choices to find out more about them. When did they happen? Are they still happening today? Who is most affected by the "binding"? Why does the "binding" happen? Write a researched essay showing your understanding of your chosen topics, and compare and contrast it to the ways the characters are bound in *Bound*. Use facts and details about the topic, and also cite the novel to support your thinking.

Your essay response to literature should follow these guidelines:

- Be at least 750 words in length.
- Cite information about the topic.
- Compare/contrast the topics to the ways Xing Xing and Wei Ping are bound.
- Cite at least three references from the novel.
- Provide a conclusion that summarizes your thoughts and findings.

Final essays are due on _____.

Name _____

Date _____

Response to Literature Rubric

Directions: Use this rubric to evaluate student responses.

	Exceptional Writing	**Quality Writing**	**Developing Writing**
Focus and Organization	☐ States a clear opinion and elaborates well. Engages readers from the opening hook through the middle to the conclusion. Demonstrates clear understanding of the intended audience and purpose of the piece.	☐ Provides a clear and consistent opinion. Maintains a clear perspective and supports it through elaborating details. Makes the opinion clear in the opening hook and summarizes well in the conclusion.	☐ Provides an inconsistent point of view. Does not support the topic adequately or misses pertinent information. Lacks clarity in the beginning, middle, and conclusion.
Text Evidence	☐ Provides comprehensive and accurate support. Includes relevant and worthwhile text references.	☐ Provides limited support. Provides few supporting text references.	☐ Provides very limited support for the text. Provides no supporting text references.
Written Expression	☐ Uses descriptive and precise language with clarity and intention. Maintains a consistent voice and uses an appropriate tone that supports meaning. Uses multiple sentence types and transitions well between ideas.	☐ Uses a broad vocabulary. Maintains a consistent voice and supports a tone and feelings through language. Varies sentence length and word choices.	☐ Uses a limited and unvaried vocabulary. Provides an inconsistent or weak voice and tone. Provides little to no variation in sentence type and length.
Language Conventions	☐ Capitalizes, punctuates, and spells accurately. Demonstrates complete thoughts within sentences, with accurate subject-verb agreement. Uses paragraphs appropriately and with clear purpose.	☐ Capitalizes, punctuates, and spells accurately. Demonstrates complete thoughts within sentences and appropriate grammar. Paragraphs are properly divided and supported.	☐ Incorrectly capitalizes, punctuates, and spells. Uses fragmented or run-on sentences. Utilizes poor grammar overall. Paragraphs are poorly divided and developed.

The responses provided here are just examples of what the students may answer. Many accurate responses are possible for the questions throughout this unit.

Answer Key

During-Reading Vocabulary Activity—Section 1: Chapters 1–7 (page 16)

1. Wei Ping's feet should be **lamented** because they are large, which is not desirable if she is trying to find a good husband.
2. Stepmother is **stricken** by the idea because she feels widows do not remarry. She would rather starve than lose her virtue.

Close Reading the Literature—Section 1: Chapters 1–7 (page 21)

1. The flashback helps readers understand that the sisters have not had bound feet since childhood because their father did not want them to do so. It also shows that Stepmother is only concerned with Wei Ping and finding her a husband.
2. Father liked his daughters to help him with his work. He felt if he had a slave girl or hired laborer, they might "sell the secrets" of his pottery making.
3. Student responses will vary. An example response may be, *The text makes me think that Stepmother only cares about Wei Ping. She tells her husband that Xing Xing can do all the work so that Wei Ping can have her feet bound. This shows her playing favorites amongst the two girls.*
4. Father did not care about bound feet because he comes from the south where binding is not as popular. He also wanted his daughters to help him in his shop. He wanted to treat his daughters equally instead of exalting Wei Ping.

Making Connections—Lotus Feet—Section 1: Chapters 1–7 (page 22)

1. Small feet were considered beautiful, and they helped a girl find a husband.
2. The toes were broken, bent down to the bottom of the foot, and then the foot was tightly bound.
3. Examples include: plastic surgery, neck rings, and corsets.

During-Reading Vocabulary Activity—Section 2: Chapters 8–13 (page 26)

1. The **shard** of pottery is hundreds—maybe thousands—of years old and has images painted on it.
2. They visit the **shrine** because Stepmother wants to honor their ancestors in hopes they give good fortune to Wei Ping and take away bad luck.

Close Reading the Literature—Section 2: Chapters 8–13 (page 31)

1. The inference is that Stepmother is going to cut off the two biggest toes on Wei Ping's other foot. She says they can view this as an opportunity and that now her feet will be even smaller. She has Xing Xing bring her a cleaver.
2. Stepmother feels sorrow and sympathy as she rubs Wei Ping's feet and calls her "sweet baby." She seems to feel nothing as she makes her plan to cut off the other toes. Finally, she feels angry at Xing Xing for bringing the raccoon to the house and not getting the cleaver quickly.
3. Wei Ping is in so much pain, she is in shock and does not understand what Stepmother plans to do. She is crying and does not respond to or even seem to be listening as Stepmother plans to cut off her other two toes.
4. Stepmother says the raccoon attacked Wei Ping because it was a demon spirit. She accuses Xing Xing of inviting demons into decent homes.

Making Connections—Old Sayings—Section 2: Chapters 8–13 (page 32)

1. B. A person must act quickly to take advantage of a good situation.
2. D. Taking care of a small problem right away is much easier than waiting until it turns into a big problem.
3. A. Trying to finish something quickly is not the best way to accomplish a task.
4. E. Getting a good start to a project means a lot of the work is already finished.
5. C. Using kind words will help a person more than being harsh.

Close Reading the Literature—Section 3: Chapters 14–17 (page 41)

1. The officials quickly choose the ugly jars as Xing Xing's work, showing they do not think a girl could do quality calligraphy. When the mark isn't copied correctly, the official says that is what is to be expected from a girl.
2. Student responses will vary. An example response may be, *He probably doesn't believe the saying because he is the one who taught her. He is simply trying to help Xing Xing.*

Answer Key

3. Xing Xing does not like or agree with the statement. It makes her angry. When Yao Wang is talking, she feels as though he has slapped her.

4. The new emperor seems to be accepting of all people. The official says the emperor would be aghast if poverty was considered a crime and that the emperor values unity over pride.

Making Connections—Section 3: Chapters 14–17 (page 42)

Student responses may include:

Health Problem	Home Remedy
headache	drink water, lie down, hot compress on head
sore throat	suck on hard candy, gargle with salt water
twisted ankle	put ice on it, elevate it, wrap it up tightly
burn	run cold water on it
can't sleep	read, do deep breathing, drink warm milk

During-Reading Vocabulary Activity—Section 4: Chapters 18–23 (page 46)

1. Xing Xing feels the fish is a **reincarnation** because it eats from her fingers, follows Xing Xing on her journey, and stays with her as she swims. She feels so much love for the fish and realizes it is her mother.

2. Xing Xing feels **dissociated** as she realizes Stepmother has likely killed the reincarnation of Xing Xing's mother.

Close Reading the Literature—Section 4 Chapters 18–23 (page 51)

1. Xing Xing thinks Stepmother wore her dress to the pool and lured the fish to her. Catching and killing the fish would have made Stepmother get wet.

2. Xing Xing wants Stepmother to feel the same pain of loss that she feels. If Wei Ping knows, she will be angry at her mother. Then, Stepmother will lose the love of the only person she cares about.

3. Instead of feeling guilty that she has not visited her father's grave that day, Xing Xing feels confident his spirit is leading her. She confronts Stepmother about her wet dress. The passage ends with Xing Xing promising to be relentless.

4. Student responses will vary. An example may be, *Stepmother did not confess. She avoided answering Xing Xing. She says, "fine it was wet" only to quiet Xing Xing, and she asks, "Have you gone mad?" when asked what knife she used.*

Close Reading the Literature—Section 5 Chapters 24–29 (page 61)

1. Stepmother and Wei Ping try to act impressive with their formal bows, but they look like they do not know what to do. Xing Xing sits on the *kang*, refusing to be formal, but her mind is sharp and clear.

2. Xing Xing thinks the prince is using the shoe as an excuse to find the girl who pleases him the most. She believes it is an unkind trick to pull on all the women who will try on the shoe.

3. Xing Xing feels like a strong woman even though society will not accept her. She realizes she can marry the prince by showing that she has the other shoe. She has begun to reach the true understanding—the *qi*—her father taught her about.

4. The prince is young. He is not very tall or fat. His clothes are padded to make him look bigger, and therefore wiser. While he looks pleasant, there is nothing that seems special about him.

Comprehension Assessment

1. B. something meant to trick people
2. H. "The prince was supposed to choose a wife by using a shoe. But, surely, many women's feet would fit that shoe."
3. Women were not appreciated or valued.
4. B. The Kong Fu Zi teaches it is a virtue for women to have a lack of talent.; C. Stepmother will raise Wei Ping's second son as a male heir for Xing Xing's father.
5. C. A woman can be more than what society expects.
6. E. "She felt strong. A strong woman in a world that tried to deny the very existence of such a thing."
7. Xing Xing's father valued his daughters and did not care about the customs that were so important to others.
8. A. "I don't think Father ever cared much about riches…He loved simple things."